The Children of Lir

Written by Maire Buonocore

Illustrated by Isabelle Arsenault

OXFORD
UNIVERSITY PRESS

Chapter 1

King Lir

Many, many years ago a king named King Lir ruled in Ireland. He was strong and brave and he commanded a mighty army. He lived with his four children, one girl and three boys, and their stepmother, the Queen. King Lir loved his children very much.

The Queen only pretended to love the children. She felt jealous whenever King Lir was with them. As time passed her jealousy grew and she hated the children more and more.

"I wish they would disappear," she thought, "then King Lir would love only me."

The Queen didn't spend time helping the children to shoot arrows, ride their ponies or play their musical instruments.

Instead, while everyone was busy, she would sneak away to her secret room and practise her evil magic. No one knew that she could make potions and cast magic spells.

Sometimes she would go secretly into the woods and try her magic on small animals. One day, she turned a frog into a fish and a worm into a snail. The Queen was beginning to think dark thoughts. She decided the only way to get rid of the children was to use her magic.

In front of the King, the Queen was kind to the children. She tricked him into thinking she cared for them. In the evenings, by the fireside, she helped them to weave and told them stories about heroes of long ago. King Lir felt happy that the Queen loved his children.

Chapter 2
The magic spell

One day, news came of war. King Lir told his army to prepare for a big battle. He gathered his family together and told them that he had to go away for a while, to fight in the war. The children didn't want him to go.

The Queen wrapped her arms around the children as they sadly waved goodbye to their father.

"I'm sure he'll be home soon," she said. "We'll have a lovely time. Why don't we go for a picnic together tomorrow?"

The next day was warm and sunny. The Queen said, "Let's go for our walk through the woods. We can have our picnic by the lake." As the children ran and skipped along the woodland path the Queen grinned.

"Good," she thought, "today I'll put my plan into action."

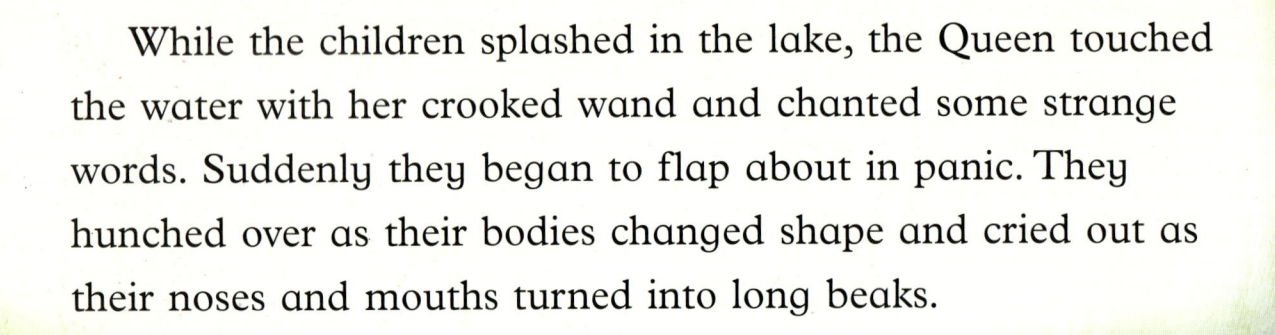

While the children splashed in the lake, the Queen touched the water with her crooked wand and chanted some strange words. Suddenly they began to flap about in panic. They hunched over as their bodies changed shape and cried out as their noses and mouths turned into long beaks.

The children looked at each other in horror. The Queen screeched with laughter, "I've changed you into swans. Now King Lir will love only me!" The Queen began to chant:

"*Now as swans you're doomed to roam, you'll never return to your father's home …*"

"From north to south, from east to west, there'll be no place for you to rest.
There's just one thing to break this spell. The chiming of a wedding bell,
For a bride and groom who must unite, from kingdoms that forever fight."

She laughed as she left them all alone.

Chapter 3
King Lir comes home

At first the children were frightened and confused. Then they began to feel sad and very lonely. They tried to speak but they couldn't. They flapped their heavy wings and stretched their strange, long necks. They had to get used to their new form and learn to fly and move as swans do.

They knew that the spell meant that they couldn't go home to the castle. The sister remembered a sad song and she began to hum the tune. As she hummed the other swans moved closer to hear her.

The other swans began to hum too. Then they began to sing words. They found they could use their human voices to sing, but not to speak. They were excited. They sang to one another telling each other how they felt about being swans.

A few weeks later King Lir and his army won the battle and came home.

"Where are the children?" he asked.

The Queen told him, "The children are staying with my cousins who live over in the west." King Lir was not happy when he heard this.

King Lir thought about his children every day. One day he was walking by the lake and he saw the four beautiful swans. The swans saw their father. They flapped their wings and moved quickly towards him. He heard their voices calling to him in song.

King Lir sat under a tree and listened as the four children sang their unhappy story. He stroked their necks and smoothed their ruffled feathers. His heart was filled with sorrow and he was extremely angry with the wicked Queen.

The swans sang, "We'll fly from lake to lake and from shore to shore, and keep on travelling until the spell is broken, but we promise we'll come to this lake whenever we return to this part of Ireland."

This pleased King Lir.

King Lir was red-faced with anger at the Queen.

"You wicked person," he shouted. "You've turned my children into swans!"

"Don't be silly, my love!" said the Queen. "They are with my cousins."

"Don't lie to me!" he yelled. "They told me themselves!"

"They can't have told you," she screamed, "they're not able to speak!"

"No, but they are able to sing," he answered. "I know everything you did."

"You loved them more than you loved me," she said softly.

King Lir raged, "Give me your wand, leave my kingdom and never come back."

Chapter 4
The storm at sea

The Queen left the castle. King Lir rode out to the high cliffs and threw the crooked wand far out into the sea. The sea became rough and the waves grew high. They began to crash against the cliffs. Above him, dark stormy clouds began to gather.

As the King destroyed the wand, the swans were flying over the sea. They flew into the storm. They were frightened. How could they fly in the storm? The wind was too strong. The rain lashed down. Lightning flashed and thunder crashed.

"We'll be separated in this storm," sang the sister. "Stay together if you can. After the storm, we'll meet at Seal Rock." The waves washed over the swans and they were all separated. The crashing thunder was louder than their voices. They all feared they would drown.

The sister arrived at Seal Rock first. She waited for her brothers. Soon a second weary and wave-washed swan arrived. The sun began to shine. The storm had passed.

Suddenly, they saw two grey shapes come flying towards Seal Rock. The four swans were delighted. They were together again.

For many years the swans travelled on. One day, they rested at the ruins of their castle.

"This used to be our home. We played here when we were children," sang one brother. There was nothing there now, no people and no animals; nettles grew in the old wheat fields. Sadly, the swans flew on.

Chapter 5

The journey ends

Soon the children passed the lake where the Queen had transformed them. From an island in the middle of the lake came delicate music. They flew closer, drawn to the sound. They saw a hermit playing on a flute. He had some silver chains beside him.

"Are you the children of Lir?" he asked.

"We are," they sang, "but who are you?"

"I'm here to take care of you. Your father wanted you to have a place where you could stop and rest. He thought you would return here one day. Years ago, he had these magic chains made to protect you."

The swans allowed themselves to be chained. Now they had a home where they lived happily with the hermit.

One day, news came of a wedding between a prince and a princess from kingdoms which were always at war. The swans sang, "At last this awful spell will be broken!"

The swans waited keenly for the wedding day. They sang together in excitement, remembering their old life. As the wedding bells chimed, the silver chains broke away, the feathers fell to the ground and the children of Lir appeared where the swans had been.

Hundreds of years had passed since the Queen had cast her spell. The children of Lir were very, very old. They lay down together in their old age and fell asleep. Now they were happy and free.

Retell the story

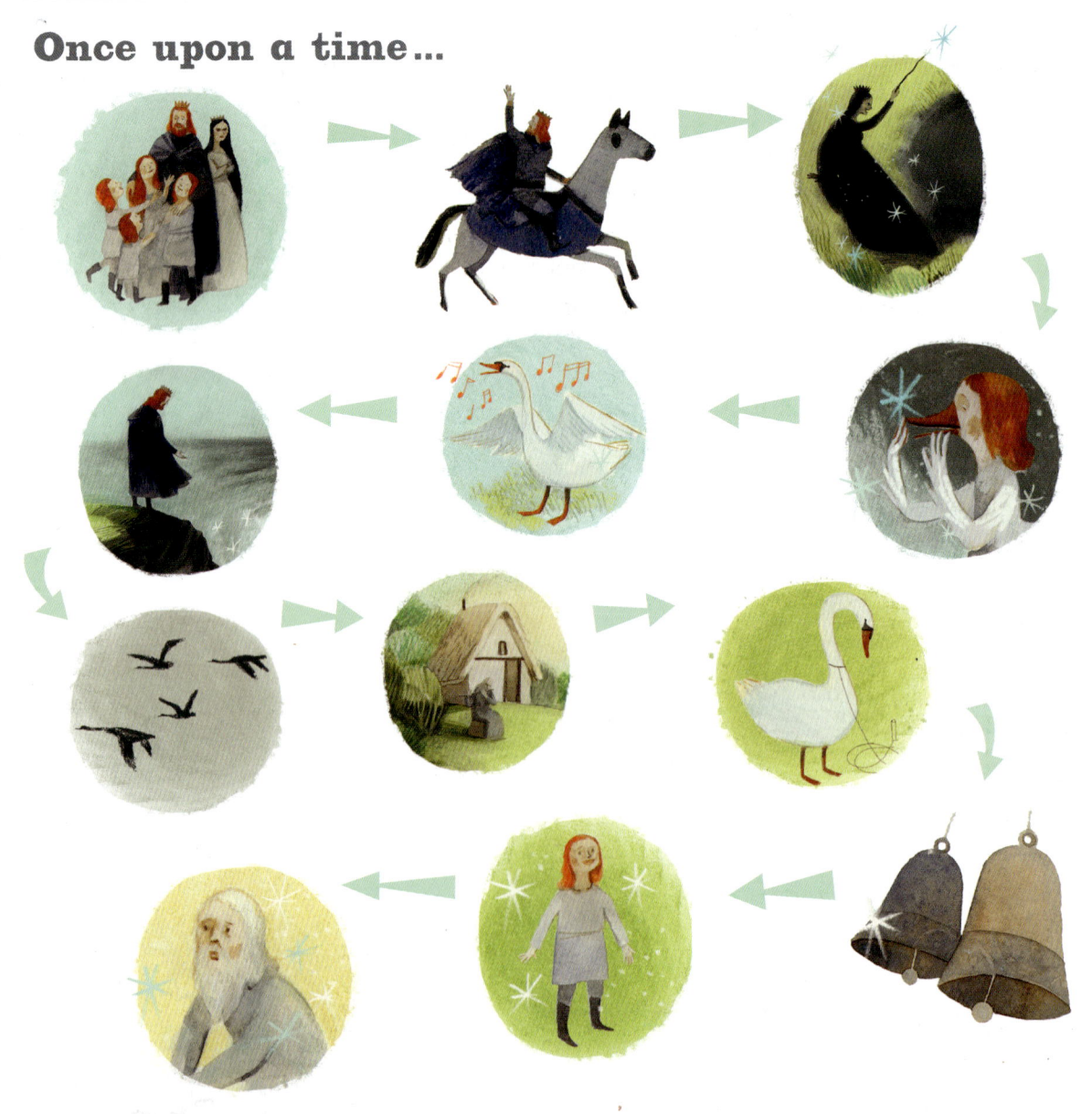

Once upon a time...

The end.